Kiki Wood

 W9-BUV-295

Kiki Wood

Jobs People Do

Christopher Maynard

A DK PUBLISHING BOOK

Text Christopher Maynard
Project Editor Penny Smith
Art Editor Claire Penny
Deputy Managing Art Editor Jane Horne
Deputy Managing Editor Mary Ling
US Editor Kristin Ward
DTP Designer Nicola Studdart
Production Kate Oliver
Picture Researcher James Clarke
Photography Steve Gorton, Dave King,
Ray Moller

Additional photography by Paul Bricknell, Geoff Brighling, Andy Crawford, Michael Crockett, Philip Dowell, Mike Dunning, Lynton Gardiner, John Garrett, Philip Gatward, Frank Greenaway, Kit Houghton, Dave Icing, Colin Keates, Bob Lang Rish, Richard Leeney, Tim Ridley, Jules Selmes, Steve Shott, Chris Stevens, Clive Streeter, Colin Walton, Alex Wilson, Peter Wilson

Second American Edition, 1997
2 4 6 8 10 9 7 5 3
DK Publishing, Inc.
95 Madison Avenue
New York, New York 10016
Visit us on the World Wide Web at http://www.dk.com

Copyright © 1997 Dorling Kindersley Limited, London

All rights reserved under International and Pan-American Copyright Conventions. No part of this publication may be reproduced, stored in a retrieval system, or transmitted in any form or by any means, electronic, mechanical, photocopying, recording or otherwise, without the prior written permission of the copyright owner.

Published in Great Britain by Dorling Kindersley Limited.

A catalog record for this book is available
from the Library of Congress.

ISBN: 0-7894-1492-9

Color reproduction by Colourscan
Printed and Bound in U.S.A. by Inland Press.

The publisher would like to thank the following for their kind permission to reproduce their photographs:
t top, b bottom, l left, r right, c center, BC back cover,
FC front cover
John Birdsall: 28tl; **Britstock-IFA:** 5c; E. Bach 31cb; **Exeter Maritime Museum** 10cl; **Robert Harding Picture Library:** 8bc, 9tl, 9c, 12tl, 25bl; **David Hoffman:** 13tr; **The Image Bank:** Barros & Barros 6tl; Jeff Cadge 20cb; G. Colliva 16tl; Ocean Images Inc 11bl; Terje Rakke 11tl, 31ca; Michael Salas 24tl; Alvis Upitus 18cl; Weinberg Clark 18bl; **Images:** 7tl **L.A.T. Photographic:** 29bl, 29tl; **Magnum Photos:** B.Barbey 19cb; **Pictor:** 7c, 9bl, 10bc, 11cl, 14tl, 17bl, 22c; ©Renault: 29c; **Rex:** 8c, 23bl; Sipa Press 5tr; **Tony Stone Images:** 22tl, 30tl; Bruce Ayres 6bl, 7bl, 26bc; Brian Blauser 4c; Paul Chesley 17tl; Robert E. Daemrich 13cl; Charles Gupton 8tl; Frank Herholdt 21cb; Bruno de Hogues 16cb; Kevin Horan 28tr; Arnulf Husmo 10c, 27c; Patrick Ingrand 16bl; Fernand Ivaldi 15tr; Chris Kaporka 16cl; Richard Kaylin 4tl; Alan Klehr 27bl; Jonathan Nourok 25cl; Steve Outram 10clb; Tony Page 28cl; Jon Riley 26tr; Michael Rosenfeld 15cla, 21tl, 28bl; Andy Sacks 23ca; Michael Thersiquel 10tl; Bob Thomas 12tr; Richard Todd 22bl; Tom & Pat Valenti 14bl; Terry Vine 14cb; Mark Wagner 17c; **Telegraph Colour Library:** 7bc, 13cb, 18tl, 20tl, 21cl, 25tr, 26c; L.Lefkowitz 6tc; Tony Ward 15c; Neal Wilson 6cl; © **Wake-Upp Productions:** Gérard Planchenault 29c; **Zefa:** 20cla, 24cl, 24c

In addition, DK would like to thank the following people and organizations for their assistance in the production of this book:
Barbara Owen (for making outfits); Bonpoint, Moss Bros (for clothes); Ocean Leisure (for diving equipment); Hollie Almeida, Cameron Blundell, Holly Franklin, Cameron Nisbett, Alexander Peter, Siána Scott, Rachelle See, Lauren Shons, Matthew Stahl, Shana Swash, Natasha Tuke, Sahil Udhian, John Vella, Peter Vella (for modeling)

Contents

Firefighter

I am a firefighter. My job is to put out fires and save people from burning buildings. When there is an emergency, I quickly put on my fireproof clothes, jump in the fire truck, and race to the scene. Then I soak the blaze with water or foam.

Helmet to protect head and neck

Fire ax to break open doors

Clothing made of material that won't burn or melt

Fireproof boots tipped with steel

Airport emergency
Foam is used on airport fires. Water doesn't work on fuel, and there is a lot of fuel at airports.

Putting out a fire
Powerful jets of water are pumped from fire hoses so fires can be fought from a safe distance.

Safety clothing
Firefighters are protected from sparks by their wide-brimmed helmets and long coats.

Ladder truck
The ladder is used to fight fire in tall buildings. It pulls out up to three times the length you see on the truck. Switches and handles on the side of the truck control the ladder and hoses.

4

Police officer

I am a police officer, so I protect people. When an offense is committed, I interview witnesses and try to find out who to arrest. When there is a car accident, I get the traffic flowing again. Every day as I patrol my beat, I talk to local people so that I know what is going on in my district.

Walkie-talkie radio to stay in touch with headquarters

Handling crowds
The police control crowds so members of the public don't block traffic or get trampled and hurt.

Patrol bike
Traffic patrol police have fast motorcycles to get through traffic blocking busy roads.

Patrol car
Police officers drive patrol cars with flashing lights to warn people to stay out of the way.

Road safety
All children must learn how to cross the road safely. A local police officer may show groups of children how to use a pedestrian crossing properly.

Mounted patrol
Police sometimes patrol on big, well-trained horses. When they are near crowds, they can see over all the heads, and if any trouble starts, they can signal to each other.

5

Surgeon

Germ barrier
Surgeons wear face masks so they don't spread germs.

scalpel

scissors

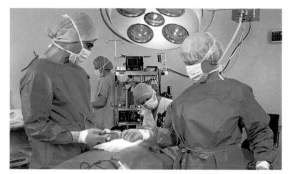

In the operating room
Teams of surgeons perform operations in operating rooms. Here they do work such as taking out tonsils and repairing injuries caused by car accidents.

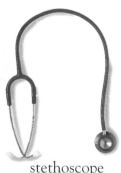

stethoscope

Being examined
Family doctors may examine you in their office, or come to your home if you are especially sick. A stethoscope helps them hear if anything is wrong with your heart.

I am a special kind of doctor called a surgeon. I use tools, including scalpels, to operate on patients in the hospital. Patients are given drugs called anesthetics, so they sleep comfortably while I repair the damage inside their bodies.

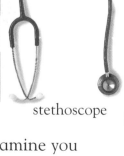

Bare bones
X-ray pictures let doctors see inside the body.

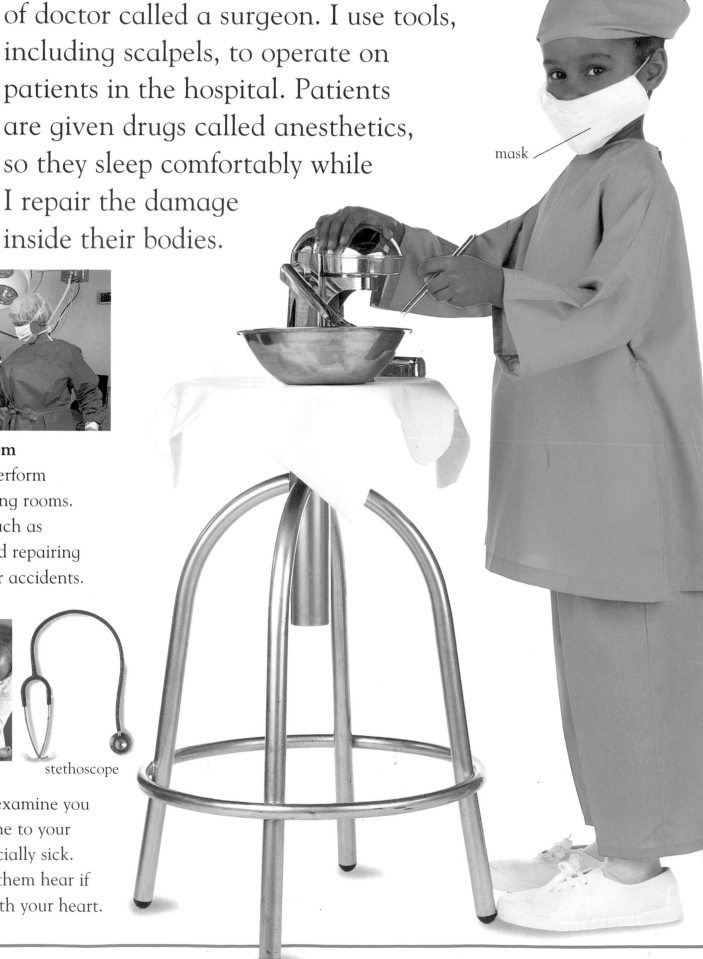

mask

At the hospital
Nurses make rounds throughout the day and night to check on their patients.

Nurse

antiseptic cream

thermometer

medicine

bandages

I am a nurse in a hospital. When people are sick, they rest and get better in the rooms where I work. I care for them by making them comfortable in bed and giving them medicine that the doctor has prescribed.

air ambulance

Paramedic

I am a paramedic and I treat people when they have been in an accident. I put them on a stretcher and take them to the hospital in an ambulance.

Passing on information
Nurses keep notes on patients so that other nurses know what treatment they've received and how they are doing.

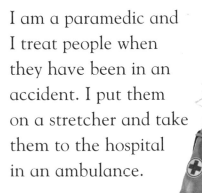

First aid
In an emergency, paramedics check to see if a person is breathing. Sometimes they give oxygen through a mask.

Say "ahh"
If a student doesn't feel well, the school nurse may check for a high temperature using a thermometer.

vegetables

Chef

In the kitchen
All the ingredients are prepared early in the day. This way chefs can cook quickly, so customers don't have to wait long for their meals to arrive.

I am a chef and I run my own restaurant. Every morning, bright and early, I go to the market to buy fresh food. Back in my kitchen, I chop and slice ingredients, preparing everything to make up the meals on my menu. I often work until late at night, cooking and serving food.

Baker

I am a baker and I work in a busy bakery. I make bread, and dozens of delicious cookies and cakes. I always start very early in the morning, so people can buy hot, fresh bread from me when they get up and start their day.

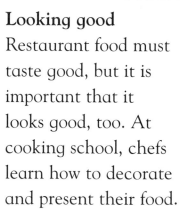

Looking good
Restaurant food must taste good, but it is important that it looks good, too. At cooking school, chefs learn how to decorate and present their food.

basket of bread

Hot from the oven
Bakers cook hundreds of loaves each week. The bread turns golden brown when it is cooked.

Waiter

I am a waiter and I serve food in a restaurant. I set the tables with cutlery, plates, and glasses. Then, when customers arrive, I show them to their tables. I give them the menu and write down their orders on my pad. When their food is ready, I serve it to them. Later, I clear away the dirty plates and present the bill.

Summer job
Some restaurants have terraces where customers can eat outside. Waiters are busy all day, pouring drinks and serving meals to guests.

Waitress

I am a waitress and I work in a big hotel. During the afternoons I serve coffee, drinks, and lots of different sandwiches and light food. I am always polite to my customers.

Wine and dine
Tables at fancy restaurants have to be reserved in advance. The food and wine is very expensive.

What can I get you?
Waiters often speak several languages so they can talk to customers from different countries. They know the menu and recommend dishes the chef does well.

Set the table
Waiters know how to set tables with the right knives, forks, and spoons for each course.

Fisherwoman

Storing fish
When the boat docks, the fish are packed in ice to keep them fresh.

I am a fisherwoman and I catch fish for people to eat. I drop nets over the sides of my boat to pull in hundreds of fish, and then store them until I reach land. It can be rough at sea, but I love being on the water.

Hat keeps off wind and spray.

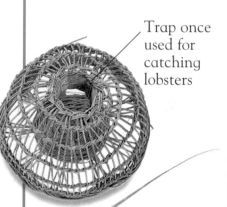

Trap once used for catching lobsters

lobster

flounder

At sea
Fishing boats are often small, and packed with nets and tackle. They can withstand gentle waves, but return to land if a bad storm approaches.

The fish market
Fish are sorted by type, then sold to stores and restaurants.

Mending nets
Fishing nets often get torn at sea, so there is always plenty of repair work for the crew to do.

fisherwoman's boots

Rubber boots keep feet dry.

Diver

I am a deep-sea diver. I wear a wet suit every time I dive because the water deep down in the ocean is very cold. I take oxygen tanks to help me breathe. Sometimes I take tools with me so I can do repairs.

Rig workers
Some divers are based on oil rigs. They work on pipes and valves under the ocean.

Hidden treasure
Divers may look for treasure in an old wreck, or even a city lost under the waves.

Undersea explorer
Submersibles are designed to dive much deeper than humans. They are used to explore the seabed.

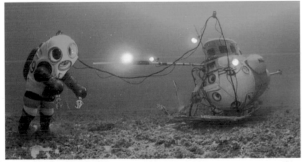

Steel helmets
Divers wear helmets deep in the ocean to keep their heads from being squashed by the water pressure.

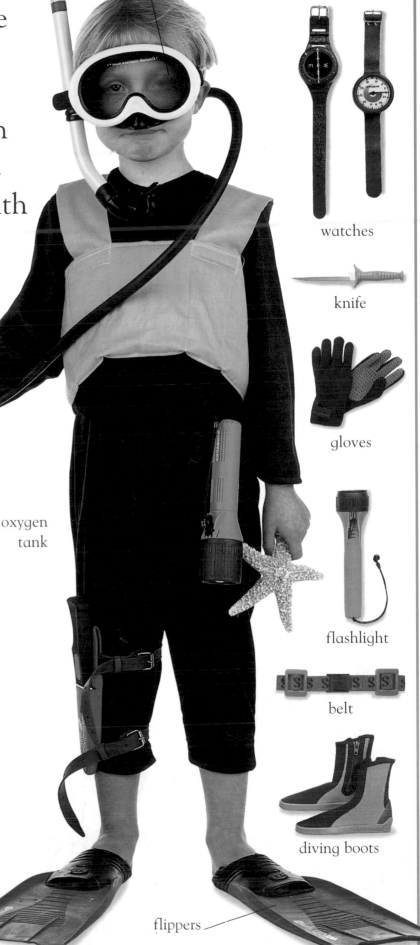

goggles

oxygen tank

flippers

Diving tools
A diver needs a lot of equipment. It includes:

watches

knife

gloves

flashlight

belt

diving boots

Photographer

I am a photographer and I take the pictures that you see in magazines and newspapers. Sometimes I photograph big parties and weddings, or I work in a studio with lights and a model. When I've got time, I like to develop my own film.

Moving pictures
A photographer who takes pictures for TV or the movies is called a cameraperson and may film all over the world.

Working in a studio
Photographs are often taken in a studio. This is so the photographer can get exactly the right lighting effects.

flash

camera

film

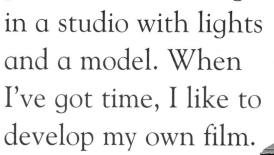

lenses

A tripod keeps the camera steady.

Tools of the trade
Cameras can be fitted with a flash and lenses. They take bright or dark pictures, color or black-and-white shots.

Sports photography
Newspaper photographers go to all the big sports events. They try to capture action shots, and use long lenses so they can get close-up pictures from far away.

Reporter

I work for a newspaper as a sports reporter. Every day, I watch teams play and I talk to the players. I ask them about their games, about their plans for the season, or how they are doing if they've been hurt. Then I type the story on a computer. I have to work quickly – if I don't get my story in on time, it won't be printed.

News of the day
Reporters cover all types of news, from celebrity weddings to political rallies.

TV news programs
Reporters also work for TV news shows. Their stories are read to the camera by a newscaster.

Getting quotes
Reporters try to talk directly to the people who make the news. The best reporters are the ones who tell both sides of a story.

Interviews
Whether working for radio or for a newspaper, reporters like to record their interviews. This way they can be sure of just what people say to them.

Teacher

Parents' night
Teachers discuss students' progress with parents, and students present special projects.

I work in a classroom full of young children. They are lively but they work hard, and I like helping them learn new things. I teach six different subjects. I like teaching science best because we can do class experiments that help explain how the world works.

pencil

pen

compass

calculator

ruler

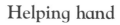

Helping hand
Teachers explain things to the whole class, but they also help just one child at a time. Reading and writing are two of the most useful things to learn.

Physical education
Children learn to play sports at school. They learn the rules of a game, and how to work together as a team. Running around also keeps their bodies fit and strong.

Story time
This is when a teacher reads the class a story and shows them the pictures. Children are encouraged to raise their hands if they want to ask a question.

14

Scientist

There are many kinds of scientists. I'm a biologist, so I work in a lab where I look for ways to cure diseases with different chemicals. If a chemical works, I make new drugs and test them carefully. Once I am sure a drug is safe, it can go on sale at a pharmacy.

Close up
Microscopes are used to look at cells that are too small to be seen by the human eye.

Studying life
Another kind of scientist is a botanist. They study how plants grow, and look for new ways to make food.

microscope

Paleontologist

I am a paleontologist. I study fossils, remnants preserved in rock, to learn about dinosaurs and other things from the past.

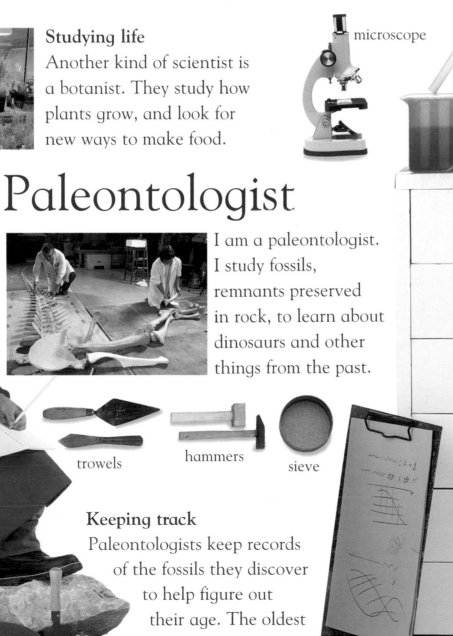

trowels

hammers

sieve

Keeping track
Paleontologists keep records of the fossils they discover to help figure out their age. The oldest dinosaur fossils found to date are over 200 million years old.

Train conductor

Bullet trains
In Japan, super-trains are called bullet trains. This is because they have rounded fronts, just like bullets. All the windows are sealed shut because the trains travel so fast. If you could open them, the air would blast in like a hurricane.

I am a train conductor. Every day I take my train up and down a route, stopping at stations to pick up passengers. Sometimes I carry cargo, such as mail, on my train, too. As I drive along, I have to watch out for signals that tell me when it is safe to go and when to stop. I always try to keep my train running on time.

train ticket

Leaving Paris
French super-trains are called TGVs. Once they leave their station in Paris, they pick up speed until they are racing along at 186 mph (300 kph). Conductors make them go, stop, and reverse. The trains steer themselves along the tracks.

Fast driver
The controls of a TGV train look a lot like those on a passenger jet. The switches and dials tell the driver that the train is running safely and that the track is clear.

Sitting comfortably
Passengers board their train from a station platform. Inside, they are often served drinks and snacks at their seats, just like in a plane. On some trains there is a restaurant where people can eat meals.

Pilot

airplane

I am a pilot and I fly planes from country to country. Sometimes I carry passengers and sometimes cargo. I know what all the dials in the cockpit mean, how to alter the plane's course, and how to put down the wheels, ready for landing. I travel all over the world and often stay in hotels.

Directing traffic
Air traffic controllers make sure airplanes don't bump into each other in the sky or when they land. They also guide planes to their parking spaces.

Coming down
Pilots talk to air traffic control over the radio. They give their positions, and ask when and where to land.

Flight attendant

I am a flight attendant and a member of the cabin crew on a passenger plane. My job is to care for passengers and make them as comfortable as possible. I tell them about safety, and show them where to find everything from headphones to magazines. I also serve them meals.

Before takeoff
Before the airplane takes off, the flight attendants go over emergency procedures and check that everyone has clicked their seat belts on tight.

Musician

Jazz instrument
Saxophones are used for jazz music. People go to clubs to hear them played by musicians.

guitar

metronome

I am a musician, a concert violinist, and I play my violin to audiences all over the world. I also record famous composers' music for CDs and television. Even when I'm not performing I have to practice every day, or else I don't play well.

conductor

Playing the violin
A violin makes music when a bow is moved across its four strings.

Orchestra at work
Up to 100 musicians sit on the stage when a symphony orchestra performs. Together they make a powerful sound that can fill the biggest concert halls. The musicians are guided through the music by a conductor. He makes sure they start playing at the right time.

trumpet

drums and cymbals

computerized keyboard

Making music last
When musicians want to record songs they go to a recording studio. They play or sing into a microphone. The songs are then recorded on tape, and copied onto CDs and cassettes.

Ballet dancer

I am a ballet dancer and I belong to a ballet company in a big city. During the day I take classes and rehearse new ballets, and some evenings I dance before a large audience. I wear beautiful costumes. I am very fit and flexible, and I can dance for hours with hardly any rest at all.

At the barre
Dancers use a barre to balance as they warm up.

In competition
Most ballroom dancers practice for months to perfect their moves.

tutu

principal dancers

ballet positions

Knowing where to stand
Each part of the stage has a name, and dancers follow stage directions. This is especially important when lots of dancers are on stage at once.

Traditional dance
Indian dancers dress in traditional costumes. When they dance, they move their heads, arms, hands, and bodies. These movements tell stories of great love or sudden and cruel death just like ballets tell a story.

Ballet shoes
Pointe shoes have stiffened tips so that dancers can dance on their toes.

Accountant

Accounting computers
Computers keep records of the money a firm spends. Records can be printed out as necessary.

Adding it up
Accountants use calculators to add up figures more quickly than they can in their heads.

I am an accountant and I work with numbers. I keep track of all the money that comes in and goes out of my company. I make sure that people who owe us money don't forget to pay. I also write the checks that pay for office equipment and the salaries of my company's employees. If a department spends too much money, I suggest cutbacks.

loose change

Lawyer

I am a criminal lawyer and I defend people who have been accused of a crime. I study the case and talk to any witnesses. Then I go to court with my clients. I try to prove my clients' innocence and keep them out of jail.

Questioning a witness
A prosecution lawyer tries to prove that a person is guilty. He needs to show why, how, and when the accused committed the crime.

Stock exchange
Hundreds of people meet to buy and sell shares at the stock exchange. Giant screens show how much the shares cost.

Stockbroker

money

I am a stockbroker and I buy and sell the shares of big companies. I try to buy shares when they are inexpensive. When the price goes up, I sell them and make a huge profit. I work hard, talking on the phone all day.

I always try to avoid mistakes. Mistakes can cost lots of money.

Trading shares
Most shares are traded by computer. Brokers work from screens that give them the latest prices. They type an order into their computer system when they want to buy or sell. It all happens very quickly.

Giving advice
Clients buy their shares with the help of an expert. But stocks can be risky; you can make money – or lose it all.

pen

calculator

Full case
Stockbrokers must know what is happening in the world of business. They often carry newspapers and company reports in their briefcases.

Springtime

Farmers plow the fields before planting. Birds will eat up any worms that the plow uncovers.

Cooped up

Chickens live in a coop and lay their eggs in straw. The eggs are collected and sold daily.

Cutting the wheat

Harvesters cut ripe wheat in a field. They separate the grain from the straw.

Farmer

I am a farmer and I work every day of the week. I keep sheep for wool and cows for milk. I also grow wheat to make into flour. I get up early and start working as soon as it is light. I feed my animals and plow my fields.

tractor and trailer

In a vineyard

Some farms grow grapes. The grapes are picked, then they are crushed and made into wine.

combine harvester

Sheep shearing

Sheeps' wool is cut off to be made into clothes and blankets. Sheep look skinny afterward.

Veterinary surgeon

I am a vet and I help sick animals. I treat cats, dogs, and other small pets in my examining room. If a cow or horse is sick, I go by car to visit it on the farm. Then I give it medicine to help it get well again.

At the vet's
Pets wait in the waiting room for the vet to see them.

Vet visits
People bring their pets to the vet in carriers so they don't run away.

Vets' instruments
Vets' instruments help them treat sick animals. Animals must stay still. To stop a dog from biting, the vet may use a muzzle.

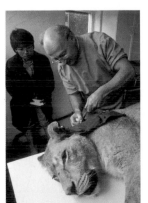

Difficult patients
Sometimes vets visit unusual patients in zoos. These animals may be too dangerous to treat when awake. Lions often have to be tranquilized first.

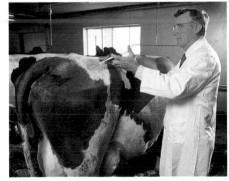

At the farm
Vets may treat whole herds of cows. To prevent an illness from spreading, the vet may inject a whole herd in one day.

A sick cat
During a checkup, the vet asks how the animal is behaving. The vet examines the animal to find out what is wrong.

Cat with bandaged leg

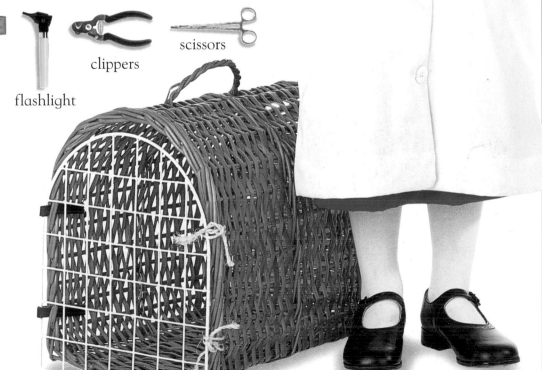

muzzle

flashlight

clippers

scissors

Mail carrier

I am a mail carrier and I deliver letters, packages, and magazines. Well before dawn, while everyone is asleep, I'm up collecting mail from the post office. I fill my bag, then go out and deliver letters street by street.

Sorting mail
Post offices sort millions of letters a day by hand and by machine.

Letters from around the world

Mailboxes
People drop their letters into mail-boxes. Each day the letters are collected and taken to the post office for sorting.

Stamps
Countries all over the world print their own stamps for people to buy.

Mail van
Letters are carried across the country in vans. When packages must be delivered the next day, they can be sent through private companies.

Garbage collector

I am a garbage collector and I drive a big truck around the city streets. I go from house to house emptying garbage pails into the back of my truck. I press a button and the garbage is crushed so that it takes up only a small space. I drive to the dump and empty my truck. I also collect newspapers and bottles that can be recycled.

At the dump
Garbage is pushed into holes. Later it will be covered with soil so plants can grow.

Other cleaning up
Oil has to be cleaned off beaches after an oil spill. This helps save wild birds and plants.

Collecting garbage
Garbage is collected weekly so it doesn't rot in the street.

Librarian

I am a librarian and I select and order books for my library. I know a lot about books and sometimes I advise people on what is good to read. I stamp books when they are borrowed, and put them in the right place on the shelf when they are returned. I also give people information about things that are happening in their neighborhood.

book

Library computers
Information can be found on computers as well as in books.

On screen
Some people copy facts onto their own computers.

Shelves of books
Libraries hold thousands of books. Books on each subject are kept together to make it easy for customers to find what they want.

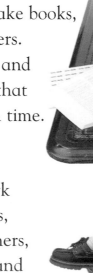

Editor

I am an editor and I make books, magazines, or newspapers. I check that the stories and pictures are right, and that everything is printed on time.

In charge
Editors work with writers, photographers, designers, and illustrators. They all help make a publication. Editors hold meetings and say who works on each project.

Designer

I am a designer, so I try to set the fashion for the year ahead. I create clothes for men, women, and children. I choose the materials the clothes are made from and how they are put together. Sometimes I organize fashion shows so my designs are seen by buyers from all over the world.

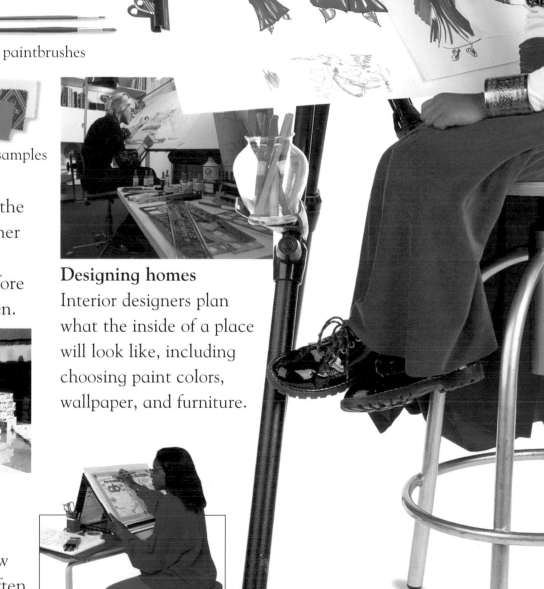

drafting table

paintbrushes

page layout

paint

fabric samples

Designing packaging
Designers also make up the way cans, boxes, and other packaging looks. They create lots of designs before the final version is chosen.

Designing homes
Interior designers plan what the inside of a place will look like, including choosing paint colors, wallpaper, and furniture.

Designing books
Graphic designers sit at drafting tables to see how a page will look. They often design on computers, too.

Mechanic

I am a garage mechanic and I fix cars when they break down or are in an accident. I give cars their regular service tune-ups, too – I always check the lights and brakes and change worn tires.

Metal repairs
Broken metal parts can be repaired by welding them together with a blowtorch.

Engine work
Sometimes an engine needs lots of work. It can be lifted out of the car to make it easier to take apart.

Mechanics' tools
Mechanics have dozens of tools and spare car parts. They use them to make repairs, tighten bolts, and get cars going.

ratchet

wrenches

multitool

spark plug

screwdriver

Cover up
Cars are sprayed with paint for an even finish. The painters wear masks, gloves, and overalls so that they don't get soaked with paint.

Other car workers
Car designers make a full-size clay model of a new car. This helps them see what their plans really look like so they can smooth out any faults.

Tires are easiest to change when you have the right tools.

Race car driver

I am a race car driver. I drive cars on race tracks and try to cross the finish line before anyone else. I drive fast, but with care – I don't want to crash. When I win, I am given a silver cup and plenty of applause. I am often interviewed for TV, too.

At the start
Races begin with the cars lined up in rows, waiting for the green signal to go. The front drivers have the best chance to win.

Pit stop
When a driver pulls in and stops during a race, his or her team of mechanics sets to work. They change all four tires and refuel the car in a matter of seconds.

Racing trucks
When trucks race they move fast, but not nearly as fast as cars.

earplugs

racing suit

gloves

boots

crash helmet

Formula 1
These cars have upside-down wings that push them onto the road to stop them from taking off at high speeds.

Builder

I am a builder and I build the houses people live in. I dig the foundations and make the outside walls from bricks. Then I put in the windows and lay the floors. One of the last things I do is plaster the inside walls.

drill

Tall buildings
Some builders put up big skyscrapers. They work high above the ground and build with steel and concrete.

hammer

screws

Plumber

I am a plumber and I work alongside builders. I fit water pipes, toilets, and tubs, and connect them to drains. I also clean out blocked pipes.

wrench

plunger

Painter

I am a painter. I decorate homes, stores, and offices. I have a van filled with cans of paints, ladders, and brushes. I put down sheets when I work so nothing is accidentally splashed.

roller

paintbrush

Painting a ship
When painters have to cover a large surface, such as the hull of a ship, they use spray guns.

Electrician

I am an electrician and I put in the wires that carry electricity around a building. I run wires beneath floors and behind walls so that all the lights work. Then I test the circuits to make sure they are safe.

wire cutters

Putting up a TV antenna
An electrician may put a TV antenna on the roof of a house. Antennae pick up signals for TV programs.

clippers

Index

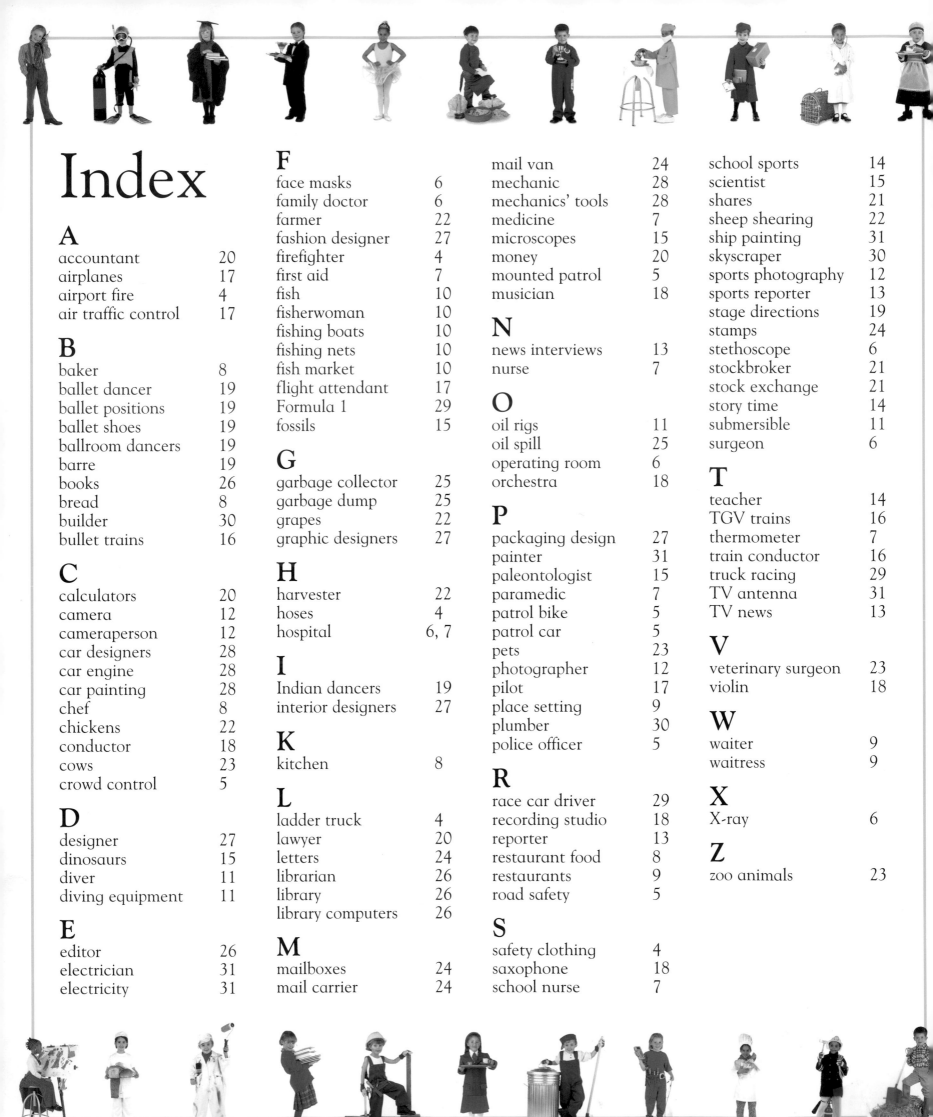